The important thing in the Olympic Games is not to win but to take part; just as the important thing in life is not the triumph but the struggle. The essential thing is not to have conquered but to have fought well.

Pierre de Coubertin

*This book lists the 1988 Olympic gold medallists and many current Olympic records. Space is provided for **you** to record the 1992 champions. Use the official abbreviations below to create your own souvenir of the 25th Olympic Games.*

AUS	Australia	GER	Germany*	POR	Portugal
AUT	Austria	HOL	Netherlands	ROM	Romania
BEL	Belgium	HUN	Hungary	SAF	South Africa
BRA	Brazil	IND	India	SUI	Switzerland
BUL	Bulgaria	ITA	Italy	SUR	Surinam
CAN	Canada	JPN	Japan	SWE	Sweden
CHN	China	KEN	Kenya	TCH	Czechoslovakia
CUB	Cuba	KOR	South Korea	TUR	Turkey
DEN	Denmark	MAR	Morocco	USA	United States of America
ESP	Spain	MEX	Mexico		
ETH	Ethiopia	NOR	Norway	URS	Soviet Union+
FIN	Finland	NZL	New Zealand	YUG	Yugoslavia†
FRA	France	PAK	Pakistan	ZAM	Zambia
GBR	Great Britain	POL	Poland		

*In the 1988 Olympics, Germany was a divided country consisting of East Germany (GDR) and West Germany (FRG).

+The Soviet Union no longer exists as a country and at the time of going to press it was unclear what would replace it.

† Yugoslavia will be represented by two teams – Croatia and Slovenia – in the 1992 Olympics.

Acknowledgments:
Photographs supplied by: Allsport – front cover bottom left, back cover, front endpaper, title page, 4-8, 14, 16, 18 centre, 19 bottom left, 20, 22-29, 32, 35 top and right, 36, 37, 45 top, 46, 49 left, 51, 54, 55; George Herringshaw (ASP) – front cover top left and right, bottom right, 10-13, 15, 17, 18 left and right, 19 top and bottom right, 21, 30, 33, 35 left, 39-42, 45 bottom, 49 right, 50, 53, 56; Tommy Hindley – 52; Eileen Langsley – 34, 35 centre; Roger Lean-Vercoe 58, 59.

Edited and compiled by Ben M Baglio.

Designed and illustrated by Chris Reed and Gavin Young.

The publishers have made every effort to ensure that the information in this book was correct at the time of publication.

A catalogue record for this book is available from the British Library.

First edition
Published by Ladybird Books Ltd Loughborough Leicestershire UK
Ladybird Books Inc Auburn Maine 04210 USA
© LADYBIRD BOOKS LTD MCMXCII
All rights reserved. No part of this publication may be reproduced, stored in a retrieval system, or transmitted in any form or by any means, electronic, mechanical, photocopying, recording or otherwise, without the prior consent of the copyright owner.

Printed in England (3)

OLYMPICS 92

The ancient Olympic Games

The first recorded Olympic Games took place at Olympia in Greece in 776 BC. They were part of a religious festival held to honour the Greek god, Zeus.

The single event at the first meeting was a race along a track 192 m (630 ft) long. Later on other events were added, including wrestling, boxing, chariot racing and a pentathlon.

The first champions at these early Games were only awarded a crown of olive leaves. However, they were often rewarded with money by the people of their home town, who were grateful for an Olympic champion.

The ancient Olympic Games continued until AD 393, when they were abolished by the Romans, who had conquered Greece. The world then had to wait over 1,500 years to celebrate the Olympic Games once more.

A Greek statue of the discus thrower, Discobolos

The modern Olympic Games – How it started

The world's greatest sporting spectacle was the idea of a French nobleman named Baron Pierre de Coubertin. During his travels round the world, Pierre de Coubertin was particularly impressed with the high interest in sports that he found in America and England.

It was after his travels that the Frenchman realised more than ever the truth of the ancient Greek ideal that the body, as well as the mind, must be cared for and improved.

He convinced many sporting authorities that an Olympic Games was an excellent means of teaching international understanding to the youth of the world. In 1896 the first Olympic Games of the modern era took place in Athens.

OLYMPIC FACTS — The first gold medal of the modern Games was won by James Connolly (USA), who won the triple jump in 1896.

Pierre de Coubertin, founder of the modern Olympic Games

The start of the 100 m final in 1896

Previous Olympic venues and dates

I	1896	Athens	April 6-15
II	1900	Paris	May 20-October 28
III	1904	St Louis	July 1-November 23
*	1906	Athens	April 22-May 2
IV	1908	London	April 27-October 31
V	1912	Stockholm	May 5-July 22
VI	1916	Berlin	Not held owing to war
VII	1920	Antwerp	April 20-September 12
VIII	1924	Paris	May 4-July 27
IX	1928	Amsterdam	May 17-August 12
X	1932	Los Angeles	July 30-August 14
XI	1936	Berlin	August 1-16
XII	1940	Tokyo, then Helsinki	Not held owing to war
XIII	1944	London	Not held owing to war
XIV	1948	London	July 29-August 14
XV	1952	Helsinki	July 19-August 3
XVI	1956	Stockholm/Melbourne	June 10-17 November 22-December 8
XVII	1960	Rome	August 25-September 11
XVIII	1964	Tokyo	October 10-24
XIX	1968	Mexico City	October 12-27
XX	1972	Munich	August 26-September 10
XXI	1976	Montreal	July 17-August 1
XXII	1980	Moscow	July 19-August 3
XXIII	1984	Los Angeles	July 28-August 12
XXIV	1988	Seoul	September 17-October 2

*1906 Games held to mark the 10th anniversary of the modern games but not numbered since they were not held in the first year of the 1904-1908 Olympiad.

This year's venue – Barcelona, Spain
July 25th – August 9th

The sports in the 1992 Olympic Games

	Page
Archery	9
Athletics	10-19
Badminton	20
Baseball	21
Basketball	22
Boxing	23-24
Canoeing	25
Cycling	26-27
Equestrian sports	28-29
Fencing	30-31
Football (Association)	32
Gymnastics	33-35
Handball	36
Hockey	37
Judo	38
Modern pentathlon	39
Rowing	40-41
Shooting	42-43
Swimming (including Diving and Water polo)	44-50
Table tennis	51
Tennis	52
Volleyball	53
Weightlifting	54-55
Wrestling	56-57
Yachting	58-59

ARCHERY

Archery is probably the oldest sport in the world and is thought to have become an organised sport in the 3rd century AD.

← OLYMPIC FACTS →
Charlotte Dod (GBR), silver medallist in 1908, was also Wimbledon Singles Champion 5 times, won the British Ladies Golf title and represented England at hockey.

The Olympic tournament features both individual and team events for men and women. In the qualification round of the individual competition each archer must shoot nine arrows at each of four targets — placed at 90 m, 70 m, 50 m and 30 m in the men's competition and at 70 m, 60 m, 50 m and 30 m in the women's competition. The 32 competitors with the highest scores progress through to the next round, in which they each shoot 12 arrows from a distance of 70 m.

In the team event each member of the team of three shoots nine arrows at a target placed at a distance of 70 m.

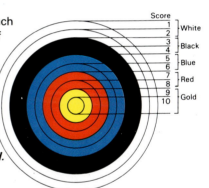

The archery tournament will take place at the *Vall d'Hebron Archery Field*.

ARCHERY...RESULTS...

Event	1988 winner	1992 winner
Men		
Individual	J Barrs (USA)	
Team	KOR	
Women		
Individual	K Soo-Nyung (KOR)	
Team	KOR	

ATHLETICS

*This is divided into **track** and **field** events.*

Track events

The track is 400 m per lap in all eight lanes. There are 'staggered' starting points for the 200 m, 400 m, 400 m hurdles, 800 m and the relays.

The 1,500 m is 3¾ laps; the 3,000 m and the 3,000 m steeplechase are both 7½ laps; the 5,000 m is 12½ laps; and the 10,000 m is 25 laps.

The 100 m, 100 m hurdles and 110 m hurdles are run on the straight.

The marathon will start in Mataró, 30 km from Barcelona, and will finish in the Olympic Stadium. The distance is 42,195 m (26 miles, 385 yards.)

Events are timed using very sensitive and accurate electronic apparatus. All races up to 10,000 m are timed and recorded to 1/100th of a second.

« OLYMPIC FACTS » Fred Lorz (USA) was disqualified as winner of the marathon in 1904 when it was discovered that he had been given a lift in a car for part of the race.

Great Britain's world champion 4 x 400 m relay team; Tokyo, 1991 (Black, Redmond, Regis and Akabusi)

Events over 10,000 m are recorded to 1/10th of a second. The marathon is recorded to the whole second.

In starting an event, the starter's commands are 'On your marks' (in the starter's native language) and, for races up to 400 m, 'set.' As soon as the competitors are still, the pistol is fired. All competitors are allowed one warning for a false start and are disqualified for a second false start, except for combined events, when two false starts are allowed.

 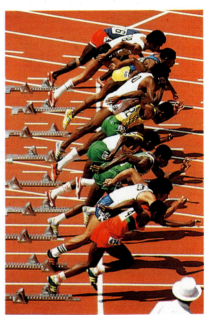

When finishing an event the winner is the first athlete to reach the finishing line with any part of his or her *torso*. (This does not include the head, arms or feet.)

During the race, competitors must stay in their allocated lane (if any). Jostling and obstructing other competitors is not allowed. The track judges will disqualify athletes guilty of these offences.

Hurdles and steeplechase

There are ten *flights* in the four hurdle events. They are 1.067 m (3 ft 6 in) high for the men's 110 m, 0.914 m (3 ft) high for the men's 400 m and 0.84 m (2 ft 9 in) for the women's 100 m. For the women's 400 m event the hurdles are 0.762 m (2 ft 6 in) high. Hurdles knocked down unintentionally do not result in disqualification. This could however make the hurdler slower.

In the steeplechase event there are 28 hurdle barriers and seven water jumps.

1 Carl Lewis (USA), gold medallist and world record holder at 100 m. He also holds the gold medal in the long jump
2 Carl Lewis sets a new 100 m world record at the 1991 World Championships
3 Yobes Ondieki (KEN), 5,000 m winner at the 1991 World Championships

TRACK EVENTS..RESULTS..

Men's events	Olympic record and time	1988 winner and time	1992 winner and time
100 m	C Lewis (USA) 9.92	C Lewis (USA) 9.92	
200 m	J DeLoach (USA) 19.75	J DeLoach (USA) 19.75	
400 m	L Evans (USA) 43.86	S Lewis (USA) 43.87	
800 m	J Cruz (BRA) 1:43.00	P Ereng (KEN) 1:43.45	
1,500 m	S Coe (GBR) 3:32.53	P Rono (KEN) 3:35.96	
5,000 m	S Aouita (MAR) 13:05.59	J Ngugi (KEN) 13:11.70	
10,000 m	B Boutayeb (MAR) 27:21.46	B Boutayeb (MAR) 27:21.46	

4 Michael Johnson (USA), world champion at 200 m

5 Noureddine Morceli (ALG), 1,500 m world champion

6 Samuel Matete (ZAM), gold medallist in the 400 m hurdles; Tokyo, 1991

4

5

6

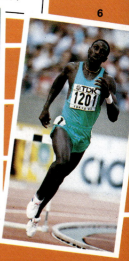

TRACK EVENTS..RESULTS.

Men's events	Olympic record and time	1988 winner and time	1992 winner and time
4 x 100 m relay	USA 37.83	URS 38.19	
4 x 400 m relay	USA 2:56.16	USA 2:56.16	
110 m hurdles	R Kingdom (USA) 12.98	R Kingdom (USA) 12.98	
400 m hurdles	A Phillips (USA) 47.19	A Phillips (USA) 47.19	
3,000 m s/chase	J Kariuki (KEN) 8:05.51	J Kariuki (KEN) 8:05.51	
20 km walk	*J Pribilinec (TCH) 1:19:57	J Pribilinec (TCH) 1:19:57	
50 km walk	*V Ivanenko (URS) 3:38:29	V Ivanenko (URS) 3:38:29	
Marathon	*C Lopes (POR) 2:09:21	G Bordin (ITA) 2:10:32	

These are best performance times since there are no records at these events.

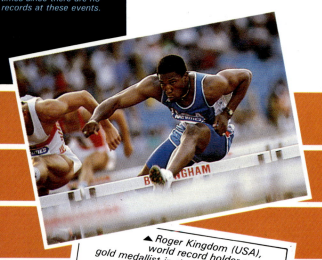

▲ Roger Kingdom (USA), world record holder and gold medallist in the 110 m hurdles
1 Katrin Krabbe (GER), 100 m and 200 m world champion
2 Debbie Flintoff-King (AUS), 1988 gold medallist in the 400 m hurdles
3 Liz McColgan (GBR), 10,000 m world champion

TRACK EVENTS..RESULTS..

Women's events	Olympic record and time	1988 winner and time	1992 winner and time
100 m	F Griffith-Joyner (USA) 10.54	F Griffith-Joyner (USA) 10.54	
200 m	F Griffith-Joyner (USA) 21.34	F Griffith-Joyner (USA) 21.34	
400 m	O Bryzgina (URS) 48.65	O Bryzgina (URS) 48.65	
800 m	N Olizarenko (URS) 1:53.43	S Wodars (GDR) 1:56.10	
1,500 m	P Ivan (ROM) 3:53.96	P Ivan (ROM) 3:53.96	
3,000 m	T Samolenko (URS) 8:26.53	T Samolenko (URS) 8:26.53	
10,000 m	O Bondarenko (URS) 31:05.21	O Bondarenko (URS) 31:05.21	
4 x 100 m relay	GDR 41.60	USA 41.98	
4 x 400 m relay	URS 3:15.17	URS 3:15.17	
100 m hurdles	Y Donkova (BUL) 12.38	Y Donkova (BUL) 12.38	
400 m hurdles	D Flintoff-King (AUS) 53.17	D Flintoff-King (AUS) 53.17	
Marathon	§ J Benoit (USA) 2:24:52	R Mota (POR) 2:25:40	

§ *Best Olympic performance.*

Field events – throwing

A qualifying standard is set for all the field events. If athletes are successful at this stage, they proceed to the final. If fewer than twelve athletes qualify, the number is made up to twelve. The finalists in the four throwing events and in the long and triple jumps have three trials. The first eight, after three trials, earn three additional trials.

Weights of implements for the throwing events are as follows:

Shot	Discus	Javelin	Hammer
Men			
7.26 kg (16 lb)	2 kg (4 lb 6.55 oz)	800 g (28.22 oz)	7.26 kg (16 lb)
Women			
4 kg (8 lb 13 oz)	1 kg (2 lb 3.27 oz)	600 g (21.16 oz)	No women's event

OLYMPIC FACTS – Ray Ewry (USA) has won more gold medals than any other competitor. He won 10 gold medals between 1900 and 1908.

Field events – jumping

In the **long jump**, the take-off board is 200 mm wide. A failure (red flag) arises if the jumper touches the ground, or makes an impression on the Plasticine beyond the far edge of the take-off board. The jump is measured from the take-off line to the nearest break in the sand made by any part of the body, including the limbs.

The **triple jump** is also known as the **hop, step and jump**. The rules are similar to the long jump except in the hopping phase. The athlete must land on the same foot as his or her take-off foot and in the 'step', land on the other foot.

Keith Connor (GBR), bronze medallist in the 1984 Olympics, showing the three phases of the triple jump – the hop, step and jump

In the **high jump** and **pole vault** events, two or more athletes often tie for first place by clearing the same height. If a tie exists, the winner is the competitor with the fewest failures at that height.

If a tie still exists, the winner is the athlete with the fewest failures at lower heights. After this, a tie is only broken for first place, in which case competitors have one attempt at the height at which they were unsuccessful. If no decision results, then the bar is lowered and raised accordingly until the tie is broken and a winner is declared.

◀ *Petra Felke (GER), javelin world record holder and 1988 Olympic gold medallist*

FIELD EVENTS..RESULTS..

Men's events	Olympic record and result	1988 winner and result	1992 winner and result
High jump	G Avdeyenko (URS) 2.38 m	G Avdeyenko (URS) 2.38 m	
Long jump	R Beamon (USA) 8.90 m	C Lewis (USA) 8.72 m	
Pole vault	S Bubka (URS) 5.90 m	S Bubka (URS) 5.90 m	
Triple jump	K Markov (BUL) 17.61 m	K Markov (BUL) 17.61 m	
Shot	U Timmermann (GDR) 22.47 m	U Timmermann (GDR) 22.47 m	
Discus	J Schult (GDR) 68.82 m	J Schult (GDR) 68.82 m	
Hammer	S Litvinov (URS) 84.80 m	S Litvinov (URS) 84.80 m	
Javelin	T Korjus (FIN) 84.28 m	T Korjus (FIN) 84.28 m	
Decathlon	D Thompson (GBR) 8,847 pts	C Schenk (GDR) 8,488 pts	

1 Sergey Bubka, pole vault world record holder and the first man to vault over 6 m

2 Javier Sotomayor (CUB), world record holder at high jump

3 Steve Backley (GBR), javelin world record holder

FIELD EVENTS ..RESULTS..

Women's events	Olympic record and result	1988 winner and result	1992 winner and result
High jump	L Ritter (USA) 2.03 m	L Ritter (USA) 2.03 m	
Long jump	J Joyner-Kersee (USA) 7.40 m	J Joyner-Kersee (USA) 7.40 m	
Shot	I Slupianek (GDR) 22.41 m	N Lisovskaya (URS) 22.24 m	
Discus	M Hellmann (GDR) 72.30 m	M Hellmann (GDR) 72.30 m	
Javelin	P Felke (GDR) 74.68 m	P Felke (GDR) 74.68 m	
Heptathlon	J Joyner-Kersee (USA) 7,291 pts	J Joyner-Kersee (USA) 7,291 pts	

4 Jackie Joyner-Kersee (USA), 1988 Olympic gold medallist at long jump and the heptathlon

5 Zhihong Huang (CHN), world champion shot putter

6 Heike Henkel (GER), world champion at high jump

BADMINTON

1992 will be the first year in which badminton is included as an Olympic sport. The competition will consist of men's and women's singles and doubles, with qualifying rounds, quarter-finals, semi-finals and finals.

The term 'badminton' comes from Badminton House in England, where the game was played by the family and guests of the Duke of Beaufort in the 19th century. The rules of the game were formalised in India during the 1870s, where the sport was popular among Army officers.

The Olympic badminton competition will be held at the **Pavello de la Mar Bella**.

"— OLYMPIC FACTS —"
Although new to the Olympics, a game similar to badminton was played in China over two thousand years ago.

BADMINTON...RESULTS...

Event	1992 winner
Men's singles	
Men's doubles	
Women's singles	
Women's doubles	

New sport

BASEBALL

Similar to the English game of rounders, baseball is actually an American invention, with the first 'diamond' laid out by Abner Doubleday in 1839. The rules of the game were drawn up in 1845 by Alexander Cartwright, Jr.

1992 marks the first time baseball is part of the official Olympic competition. There will be an eight-team men's tournament, comprising preliminary, semi-final and final matches. In the preliminary round of the competition, each team will play one match against all of the other teams.

The Olympic baseball competition will be held at two venues: the **Hospitalet Baseball Stadium** and the **Viladecans Baseball Stadium**.

"← OLYMPIC FACTS →"
Baseball has been demonstrated seven times at the Olympics. The first occasion was in 1912, when the USA beat Sweden 13-3.

BASEBALL...RESULTS...

1992 winner

Baseball was an exhibition sport at the 1988 Olympics, with the USA beating Japan in the final

New sport

BASKETBALL

In the preliminary rounds of this competition the teams are divided into two groups. Each team plays every other in the same group, and gains 2 points for a win and 1 point for a loss. In the men's competition the four teams from each group with the highest number of points go forward to the quarter-finals, while in the women's competition the top two teams from each group go on to the semi-finals. At this stage the tournament is organised on a knock-out basis.

"← OLYMPIC FACTS →"
The longest winning streak in the Olympics from 1936 to 1972, is held by the USA basketball team. It ended when they were beaten 51–50 by the Soviet Union.

BASKETBALL...RESULTS...

	1988 winner	1992 winner
Men	URS	
Women	USA	

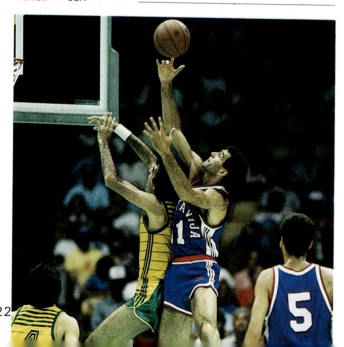

BOXING

The boxing competition involves twelve weight divisions organised on a knock-out basis. Each contest is boxed over three 3-minute rounds with a 1-minute rest between rounds. The result depends on a knock-out, the referee stopping the contest for the safety of the loser, or on a points decision.

Many Olympic boxing champions, including George Foreman, Joe Frazier and Cassius Clay (Muhammad Ali) have gone on to win world professional titles.

The venue for the boxing competition will be the **Pavello Club Joventut** in Badalona.

"— OLYMPIC FACTS —" The only brothers to win gold medals for boxing are Leon and Michael Spinks (USA).

Giovanni Parisi (ITA) being declared the winner in the 1988 featherweight division

BOXING...RESULTS...

Division	1988 winner	1992 winner
Light flyweight (Up to 48 kg)	I Hristov (BUL)	_____
Flyweight (Under 51 kg)	K Kwang-Sun (KOR)	_____
Bantamweight (Under 54 kg)	K McKinney (USA)	_____
Featherweight (Under 57 kg)	G Parisi (ITA)	_____
Lightweight (Under 60 kg)	A Zülow (GDR)	_____
Light welterweight (Under 63.5 kg)	V Janovski (URS)	_____
Welterweight (Under 67 kg)	R Wangila (KEN)	_____
Light middleweight (Under 71 kg)	P Si-Hun (KOR)	_____
Middleweight (Under 75 kg)	H Maske (GDR)	_____
Light heavyweight (Under 81 kg)	A Maynard (USA)	_____
Heavyweight (Under 91 kg)	R Mercer (USA)	_____
Super-heavyweight (Over 91 kg)	L Lewis (CAN)	_____

CANOEING

There are two types of Olympic canoeing. The *kayak* canoeist uses a paddle with a blade at each end. He must use the left-hand blade on the left side and the right-hand blade on the right side of the kayak alternately.

In *Canadian* canoeing, the paddle has one blade, which is used on each side of the canoe alternately.

"— OLYMPIC FACTS —" The fastest speed over the 1,000 m Olympic course is 19.7 km/hr, which was achieved by the K-4 team of the Soviet Union in 1980.

CANOEING...RESULTS...

Men's events	1988 winner	1992 winner
500 m		
Kayak singles (K-1)	Z Gyulay (HUN)	
Kayak pairs (K-2)	NZL	
Canadian singles (C-1)	O Heukrodt (GDR)	
Canadian pairs (C-2)	URS	
1,000 m		
Kayak singles (K-1)	G Barton (USA)	
Kayak pairs (K-2)	USA	
Kayak fours (K-4)	HUN	
Canadian singles (C-1)	I Klementyev (URS)	
Canadian pairs (C-2)	URS	
Slalom		
Kayak singles (K-1)	*New event*	
Canadian singles (C-1)	*New event*	
Canadian pairs (C-2)	*New event*	
Women's events		
500 m		
Kayak singles (K-1)	V Guecheva (BUL)	
Kayak pairs (K-2)	GDR	
Kayak fours (K-4)	GDR	
Slalom		
Kayak singles (K-1)	*New event*	

CYCLING

The cycling events are held either on the track at the **Municipal Velodrome** or on the road.

The 1,000 m time trial is held on the track. Competitors start off individually at intervals and the winner is the cyclist who records the fastest time over the course.

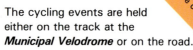

« OLYMPIC FACTS »
The longest cycling race of the Olympic Games was in 1912 when the course covered 320 km (199 miles).

The individual sprint races cover four laps of the track and are usually contested by two or three cyclists. The winner is the cyclist with the fastest time over the last 200 m of the course, the earlier parts of the race being used to gain a favourable position.

In the individual pursuit race two cyclists start at opposite sides of the track. The aim is to catch up with the opponent and if this occurs the race is over. If a competitor does not manage to catch his opponent then the cyclist who records the fastest time is the winner. A women's individual pursuit has been added to the competition this year.

The 4,000 m team pursuit involves teams of four cyclists, who compete as in the individual pursuit. Each member of the team takes it in turn to act as a pacemaker. The times of the first three cyclists in each team determine the winner.

The points race takes place over 200 laps of the track. On every eighth lap the first cyclist over the winning line gains 5 points, the second cyclist gains 3 points, the third cyclist gains 2 points and the fourth gains 1 point. The points awarded on the 100th lap and the final lap are worth double. The winner is the cyclist gaining the greatest number of points overall.

The road events are the 100 km team time trial for men, a road race for men (covering 194.4 km) and a road race for women (covering 81 km).

Colin Sturgess (GBR) in the individual pursuit; Seoul 1988 ▶

CYCLING...RESULTS...

Men's events	1988 winner	1992 winner
Sprint	L Hesslich (GDR)	
1,000 m time trial	A Kiritchenko (URS)	
100 km team time trial	GDR	
4,000 m individual pursuit	G Umaras (URS)	
4,000 m team pursuit	URS	
50 km points race	D Frost (DEN)	
Road race	O Ludwig (GDR)	
Women's events		
Sprint	E Saloumae (URS)	
3,000 m individual pursuit	*New event*	
Road race	M Knol (HOL)	

EQUESTRIAN SPORTS

Equestrian sports include individual and team competitions in show jumping, dressage and the three day event.

The events will take place at the *Royal Polo Club* and the *Circuit d'Hipica*.

"← OLYMPIC FACTS →" Because of the strict quarantine laws in Australia, the equestrian events in the 1956 Games had to be held in Stockholm, not Melbourne.

Show jumping

In the individual event competitors must jump ten to twelve obstacles in two qualifying rounds. The maximum height of the obstacles is 1.60 m (5ft 3in). The widest water jump is 4.75 m (15ft 6in) and the widest spread obstacle is 2.20 m (7ft 2½ in). Competitors with the lowest number of faults progress to the final competition, where they must jump a further two courses.

In the team event the four members of each team tackle a course similar to that in the qualifying rounds of the individual events. The twelve teams with the fewest faults then jump against the clock over six obstacles up to 1.70 m (5 ft 6¾ in) in height. Only the three best scores for each team count towards the final result.

Dressage

Dressage judges the understanding between a horse and its rider. The competition involves a variety of paces, halts, direction changes, movements and figures. Points are awarded for each skill, out of a maximum of ten. In the team competition only the scores of the three best members count towards the team score. The twelve riders with the highest scores are then allowed to take part in the individual event.

Three day event

This includes dressage, show jumping and a cross-country endurance test. The scores of the three best members are added together to give the team total.

Nick Skelton (GBR) and Apollo at the 1988 Olympics

EQUESTRIAN...RESULTS...

Event	1988 winner	1992 winner
Show jumping		
Individual	P Durand (FRA)	_____
Team	FRG	_____
Dressage		
Individual	N Uphoff (FRG)	_____
Team	FRG	_____
Three day event		
Individual	M Todd (NZL)	_____
Team	FRG	_____

FENCING

The fencing competitions include both individual and team events for men and women. Men fight with three weapons: foil, épée and sabre. Women fight with the foil only.

To score, the fencer must hit certain target areas on the opponent's body. The target areas are different for each weapon. In the qualifying rounds a fencer must score five hits to win. In later rounds, a fencer must win two out of three fights against the same opponent in order to progress through the competition.

The venue for the fencing tournament will be the **Metallurgy Hall**.

« OLYMPIC FACTS »
The only competitor ever to win gold medals at six consecutive Games is Aladar Gerevich (HUN) who competed with the sabre between 1932 and 1960.

Wires attached to each competitor electronically record hits to the target area

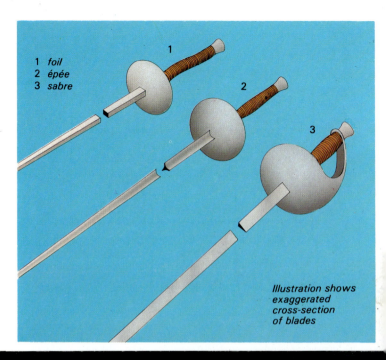

1 *foil*
2 *épée*
3 *sabre*

Illustration shows exaggerated cross-section of blades

FENCING...RESULTS...

Men's events	1988 winner	1992 winner
Individual foil	S Cerioni (ITA)	
Team foil	URS	
Individual sabre	J-F Lamour (FRA)	
Team sabre	HUN	
Individual épée	A Schmitt (FRG)	
Team épée	FRA	
Women's events		
Individual foil	A Fichtel (FRG)	
Team foil	FRG	

FOOTBALL (Association)

Only sixteen teams contest the medals at the Olympic Games in this sport. The teams are divided into groups of four with each team playing one match against each of the other teams in the group. The teams are awarded 2 points for a win, 1 point for a draw and no points for a defeat. The two teams in each group with the highest number of points qualify for the quarter-finals. The competition then becomes a knock-out tournament to decide the medal placings.

The only current regulation on players taking part in the competition is that they must have been born on or after 1 August 1969.

OLYMPIC FACTS — The first goal in Olympic competition was scored by Great Britain in their 4–0 defeat of France in 1900.

South Korea v Soviet Union; Seoul, 1988

FOOTBALL...RESULTS...

1988 winner	1992 winner
URS	

GYMNASTICS

There are eight events in the men's competition: floor exercises, pommel horse, rings, horse vault, parallel bars, horizontal bar, individual combined exercises and men's team. All competitors are given a mark out of ten for their performance in each of the events.

In the women's competition there are seven events: horse vault, uneven (asymmetric) bars, balance beam, floor exercises, individual combined exercises, women's team and rhythmic gymnastics. Again, all competitors are marked out of ten.

The gymnastics competitions will take place at the *Sant Jordi Hall* and the *Barcelona Sports Hall*.

« OLYMPIC FACTS » The first perfect score of 10 was awarded to Nadia Comaneci (ROM) in 1976.

The new Sant Jordi Hall

GYMNASTICS...RESULTS...

Men's events	1988 winner	1992 winner
Floor exercises	S Kharikov (URS)	
Pommel horse	L Gueraskov (BUL)	
	Z Borkai (HUN)	
	D Bilozertchev (URS)	
Rings	H Behrendt (GDR)	
	D Bilozertchev (URS)	
Horse vault	L Yun (CHN)	
Parallel bars	V Artemov (URS)	
Horizontal bar	V Artemov (URS)	
	V Lyukhine (URS)	
Combined exercises	V Artemov (URS)	
Team competition	URS	

1 Bilozertchev (URS), joint winner in two events
2 Valeri Belenki
3 Li Chunyang (CHN)
4 Daniela Silivas (ROM), Olympic gold medallist in three events
5 1988 team champions – URS (1st), ROM (2nd), GDR (3rd)
6 Tatiana Gutsu
7 Kim Zmeskal (USA)

GYMNASTICS...RESULTS...

Women's events	1988 winner	1992 winner
Horse vault	S Bogunskaya (URS)	
Uneven bars	D Silivas (ROM)	
Balance beam	D Silivas (ROM)	
Floor exercises	D Silivas (ROM)	
Rhythmic competition	M Lobatch (URS)	
Combined exercises	Y Chouchounova (URS)	
Team competition	URS	

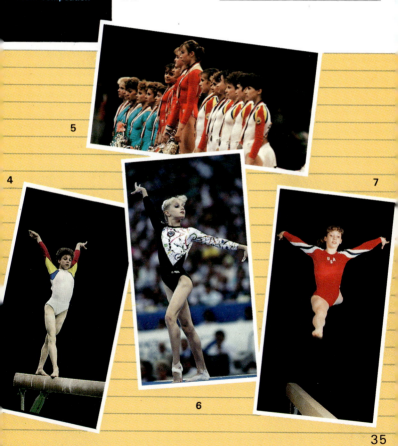

5

4

6

7

HANDBALL

Handball is a team game in which the player holding the ball is allowed to take three steps before he or she must either bounce the ball with one hand or pass it to another team member. Once the ball has been caught with two hands the player must either shoot at goal or pass the ball within three seconds. A goal is scored by throwing the ball past the keeper into the goal. Shots at goal must be made from outside the goal area.

OLYMPIC FACTS — The 1936 handball competition was played as an outdoor game with eleven players in each team.

HANDBALL...RESULTS...

	1988 winner	1992 winner
Men	URS	
Women	KOR	

HOCKEY

The game of hockey is played between two teams with eleven players in each team.

In the Olympic tournament the teams are divided into two pools and the two top teams from each pool go through to the semi-finals. The event then becomes a knock-out competition.

Each match is played over two halves which each last for 35 minutes. At the semi-final and final stages of the tournament a match that has been drawn at the end of full-time will then have extra time played. If a draw still exists then the match is decided by penalty shots.

The hockey tournament will take place at the **Terrassa Hockey Stadium**.

« OLYMPIC FACTS » Roop Singh scored the highest number of goals in an Olympic hockey match. He got 12 of India's 24 goals against the United States in 1932.

HOCKEY...RESULTS...

	1988 winner	1992 winner
Men	GBR	
Women	AUS	

Great Britain's gold medal winning hockey team at the 1988 Olympics

JUDO

The sport of judo began as a means of self-defence. To be successful at this sport the *judoka* must be well balanced, fast and strong.

The competition is organised on an elimination basis. To win a bout outright a competitor must throw their opponent cleanly onto their back or immobilise them on the ground for 30 seconds.

Women's judo was a demonstration sport at the 1988 Olympics. 1992 marks the first official Olympics judo competition for women.

«— OLYMPIC FACTS —»

Hector Rodriguez (CUB), who won the lightweight division in 1976, took up the sport to defend himself against his older brothers.

JUDO...RESULTS...

Weight class	1988 winner	1992 winner
Men's events		
Up to 60 kg	K Jae-Yup (KOR)	
Up to 65 kg	L Kyung-Keun (KOR)	
Up to 71 kg	M Alexandre (FRA)	
Up to 78 kg	W Legien (POL)	
Up to 86 kg	P Seisenbacher (AUT)	
Up to 95 kg	A Miguel (BRA)	
Over 95 kg	H Saito (JPN)	
Women's events		
Up to 48 kg	*New event*	
Up to 52 kg	*New event*	
Up to 56 kg	*New event*	
Up to 61 kg	*New event*	
Up to 66 kg	*New event*	
Up to 72 kg	*New event*	
Over 72 kg	*New event*	

MODERN PENTATHLON

When the seventeenth Olympic Games in ancient Greece finished, the war-like Spartans complained that there was not a competition that tested the all-round ability of the athletes. To answer this complaint a pentathlon was introduced at the next Games. The five events in the ancient pentathlon were discus, long jump, javelin, running and wrestling.

The five events in the modern pentathlon are show jumping (over fifteen obstacles on a 600 m course), fencing (épée), swimming (300 m freestyle), shooting (pistol or revolver at 25 m) and cross-country running (4,000 m).

OLYMPIC FACTS — Boris Onischenko (URS) was disqualified in 1976 when it was discovered that he had altered his épée to register hits without its making contact.

PENTATHLON...RESULTS...

Event	1988 winner	1992 winner
Individual	J Martinek (HUN)	
Team	HUN	

Great Britain's bronze medallists in the 1988 team event.
Left to right: Graham Brookhouse, Dominic Mahony, Richard Phelps

ROWING

The Chinese were the first to engage in the sport of long-boat racing on rivers and tidal waters. To this day Chinese festivals include races between dragon boats or shallow draft boats, 22 m (73 ft) long, moved by 27 oarsmen.

To standardise the events and equipment, many obstacles had to be overcome. This sport has probably made more progress in equipment than any other sport and it is extremely difficult to keep the competition athletic rather than technological.

No Olympic records exist for this sport as water conditions vary so much from one Games to another.

The rowing events will take place at **Banyoles Lake**, 124 km northeast of Barcelona.

«— OLYMPIC FACTS —» Vyacheslav Ivanov (URS) lost his 1956 gold medal for single sculls in Lake Wendouree when he threw it up in the air to celebrate his win.

HRH the Princess Royal presents gold medals to Steven Redgrave and Andrew Holmes (GBR); Seoul, 1988

The victorious East German double sculls team; Seoul, 1988

ROWING...RESULTS...

Event	1988 winner	1992 winner
Men (2,000 m)		
Single sculls	T Lange (GDR)	
Double sculls	HOL	
Coxless pairs	GBR	
Coxed pairs	ITA	
Coxless fours	GDR	
Coxed fours	GDR	
Quadruple sculls	ITA	
Coxed eights	FRG	
Women (2,000 m)		
Single sculls	J Behrendt (GDR)	
Double sculls	GDR	
Coxless pairs	ROM	
Coxed fours	GDR	
Quadruple sculls	GDR	
Coxed eights	GDR	

SHOOTING

The shooting tournament has a number of separate events for men and women and two open events where men and women compete together.

The open events are the *skeet* and *Olympic trap shooting*. In both cases competitors use a shotgun and fire at saucer-shaped clay targets. These targets are designed so that their flight is similar to that of a game bird at take-off. The 'game birds' are released from traps on the shooter's command. A hit is scored when the clay is visibly broken or reduced to dust.

In the running target competition the target is divided into ten rings. It is moved at a constant speed across an opening 2 m in width. Two speeds are used: a *slow run* where the target is shown for 5 seconds and a *fast run* where it is shown for 2½ seconds.

The shooting events will take place at the **Mollet Olympic Shooting Range**.

◀ *The simple trap shown is used for both Olympic skeet and trap competitions*

— OLYMPIC FACTS —
Oscar Swahn (SWE) was the Olympic's oldest competitor. He was 64 when he won his last gold medal, and 72 when he last competed.

SHOOTING...RESULTS...

Men's events	1988 winner	1992 winner
Rapid fire pistol (25 m)	A Kouzmine (URS)	
Free pistol (50 m)	S Babii (ROM)	
Air pistol (10 m)	T Kiriakov (BUL)	
Running target (10 m)	*T Heiestad (NOR)	
Smallbore – 3 positions (50 m)	M Cooper (GBR)	
Smallbore – prone position (50 m)	M Varga (TCH)	
Air rifle (10 m)	G Maksimovic (YUG)	
Women's events		
Sport pistol (25 m)	N Saloukvadze (URS)	
Air pistol (10 m)	J Sekaric (YUG)	
Air rifle (10 m)	I Chilova (URS)	
Smallbore – 3 positions (50 m)	S Sperber (FRG)	
Open events		
Trap	D Monakov (URS)	
Skeet	A Wegner (GDR)	

In 1988 the event was called Running game (50 m)

Prone position

Standing position

Kneeling position

◄ *Malcolm Cooper (GBR), 1984 and 1988 gold medallist*

SWIMMING

The swimmers compete using four different strokes: breaststroke, backstroke, butterfly and freestyle (usually the crawl). Medley races consist of each of the four strokes swum over four equal distances.

The fastest qualifying swimmer swims in the final in lane four (centre), the next quickest lane five, then three and so on. This explains the arrowhead formation when viewed on TV.

In the synchronised swimming competition for women there are both solo and duet events. Competitors must first complete four figures with various degrees of difficulty. They then perform a free routine to music lasting 3½ minutes in the solo event and 4 minutes in the duet event.

«— OLYMPIC FACTS —»
Johnny Weissmuller (USA), who won five freestyle events, went on to star in many "Tarzan" films.

SWIMMING...RESULTS...

Men's events	Olympic record and time	1988 winner and time	1992 winner and time
Freestyle			
50 m	M Biondi (USA) 22.14	M Biondi (USA) 22.14	
100 m	M Biondi (USA) 48.63	M Biondi (USA) 48.63	
200 m	D Armstrong (AUS) 1:47.25	D Armstrong (AUS) 1:47.25	
400 m	U Dassler (GDR) 3:46.95	U Dassler (GDR) 3:46.95	
1,500 m	V Salnikov (URS) 14:58.27	V Salnikov (URS) 15:00.40	
Backstroke			
100 m	D Suzuki (JPN) 55.05	D Suzuki (JPN) 55.05	
200 m	R Carey (USA) 1:58.99	I Polianski (URS) 1:59.37	
Breaststroke			
100 m	S Lundquist (USA) 1:01.65	A Moorhouse (GBR) 1:02.04	
200 m	V Davis (CAN) 2:13.34	J Szabo (HUN) 2:13.52	
Butterfly			
100 m	A Nesty (SUR) 53.00	A Nesty (SUR) 53.00	

SWIMMING...RESULTS...

Men's events	Olympic record and time	1988 winner and time	1992 winner and time
Butterfly			
200 m	M Gross (FRG) 1:56.94	M Gross (FRG) 1:56.94	
Individual medley			
200 m	T Darnyi (HUN) 2:00.17	T Darnyi (HUN) 2:00.17	
400 m	T Darnyi (HUN) 4:14.75	T Darnyi (HUN) 4:14.75	
Medley relay			
4 x 100 m	USA 3:36.93	USA 3:36.93	
Freestyle relay			
4 x 100 m	USA 3:16.53	USA 3:16.53	
4 x 200 m	USA 7:12.51	USA 7:12.51	

1 Adrian Moorhouse (GBR), Olympic champion and world record holder for 100 m breaststroke

2 Matt Biondi (USA), winner of five gold medals, a silver and a bronze at the 1988 Olympics

SWIMMING...RESULTS...

Women's events	Olympic record and time	1988 winner and time	1992 winner and time
Freestyle			
50 m	K Otto (GDR) 25.49	K Otto (GDR) 25.49	
100 m	B Krause (GDR) 54.79	K Otto (GDR) 54.93	
200 m	H Friedrich (GDR) 1:57.65	H Friedrich (GDR) 1:57.65	
400 m	J Evans (USA) 4:03.85	J Evans (USA) 4:03.85	
800 m	J Evans (USA) 8:20.20	J Evans (USA) 8:20.20	
Backstroke			
100 m	R Reinisch (GDR) 1:00.86	K Otto (GDR) 1:00.89	
200 m	K Egerszegi (HUN) 2:09.29	K Egerszegi (HUN) 2:09.29	
Breaststroke			
100 m	T Dangalakova (URS) 1:07.95	T Dangalakova (URS) 1:07.95	
200 m	S Hörner (GDR) 2:26.71	S Hörner (GDR) 2:26.71	

1 K Egerszegi (HUN), gold medallist at 200 m backstroke
2 Janet Evans (USA), Olympic record holder at 400 m and 800 m freestyle
3 Catherine Plewinski (FRA)
4 Kristin Otto (GER), winner of six gold medals at the 1988 Olympics
5 Daniela Hunger (GER)

SWIMMING...RESULTS...

Women's events	Olympic record and time	1988 winner and time	1992 winner and time
Butterfly			
100 m	K Otto (GDR) 59.00	K Otto (GDR) 59.00	
200 m	M Meagher (USA) 2:06.90	K Nord (GDR) 2:09.51	
Individual medley			
200 m	D Hunger (GDR) 2:12.59	D Hunger (GDR) 2:12.59	
400 m	P Schneider (GDR) 4:36.29	J Evans (USA) 4:37.76	
Medley relay			
4 x 100 m	GDR 4:03.74	GDR 4:03.74	
Freestyle relay			
4 x 100 m	GDR 3:40.63	GDR 3:40.63	
Synchronised swimming			
Solo	No record	C Waldo (CAN)	
Duet	No record	CAN	

4

5

DIVING

The diving competition consists of the springboard and platform (highboard) events.

The number of dives which each competitor performs is eleven for men's springboard, ten for women's springboard and men's platform and eight for women's platform.

Each dive is marked out of ten by the judges, based on how well the dive is performed. The highest and lowest marks are discounted and the remainder are added together and multiplied by a tariff value which varies according to how difficult the dive is.

Five basic dives. All other dives are derived from these ▶

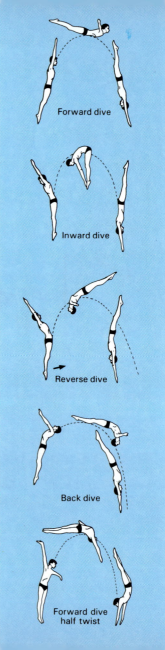

Forward dive

Inward dive

Reverse dive

Back dive

Forward dive half twist

OLYMPIC FACTS
Marjorie Gestring (USA) is the youngest individual gold medallist. She won the 1936 springboard title when she was 13 years 268 days.

Greg Louganis (USA), winner of the springboard and platform events in 1984 and 1988

Xu Yanmei (CHN), platform gold medallist

DIVING...RESULTS...

Men's events	1988 winner	1992 winner
Springboard	G Louganis (USA)	
Platform	G Louganis (USA)	
Women's events		
Springboard	G Min (CHN)	
Platform	X Yanmei (CHN)	

WATER POLO

Water polo is a demanding team game played by two teams of seven players, one of whom is the goalkeeper. The competition will take place in a pool measuring 33.3 m x 25 m (109 ft x 82 ft).

The game itself is divided into four 5-minute periods. The object of the game is to pass the ball and to throw it into the goal of the opposing team.

The twelve teams taking part in the competition are divided into two groups. Each team plays every other team in their group and the top two teams from each group then play in a knock-out competition to decide the medal winners.

"— OLYMPIC FACTS —"
The 1936 water polo match Hungary v Soviet Union had to be abandoned when the referee decided it was becoming "a boxing match underwater".

WATER POLO...RESULTS...

	1988 winner	1992 winner
Men	YUG	

TABLE TENNIS

This fast-paced game was introduced as an official Olympics event in 1988.

There are singles and doubles events for both men and women. The competitions are organised on a group basis for the first round. The highest placed players or pairs in each group then go on to compete in play-off matches to determine the final places.

Matches are the best of three games in the groups stage and the best of five games in the knock-out stages.

TABLE TENNIS...RESULTS...

Event	1988 winner	1992 winner
Men's singles	Y Nam-Kyu (KOR)	
Men's doubles	CHN	
Women's singles	C Jing (CHN)	
Women's doubles	KOR	

TENNIS

Tennis was reintroduced as an official Olympic event in 1988. (Except for two exhibition tournaments, it had been suspended since 1924.)

OLYMPIC FACTS — The first female competitor to win an Olympic gold medal was Charlotte Cooper (GBR), who won the tennis competition in 1900.

The tennis tournament consists of the following events: men's singles, men's doubles, women's singles and women's doubles.

Matches for men are the best of five sets and matches for women are the best of three sets. Tie-breaks operate in every set except the final one, where play must continue until one player or pair leads by two clear games.

The tennis matches will be played at the **Vall d'Hebron Tennis Park**.

Steffi Graf (FRG) with her gold medal in the women's singles competition; Seoul, 1988

TENNIS...RESULTS...

Event	1988 winner	1992 winner
Men's singles	M Mecir (TCH)	
Men's doubles	USA	
Women's singles	S Graf (FRG)	
Women's doubles	USA	

VOLLEYBALL

This game involves six players in each team and is played on a court with a high net across the centre.

OLYMPIC FACTS — Between 1964 and 1980 the men's team from the Soviet Union lost only 4 of its 39 matches and the women's team was defeated only twice in 28 matches.

The aim of the game is to return the ball over the net before it touches the ground. Each team may touch the ball up to three times before it must go over the net to the opposition. Points are obtained when the opposing team either hits the ball out of court or fails to return it before it touches the ground. Points are only given to the serving team and if the serving team is penalised the service then passes to the opposition.

Each match is the best of five sets. A set is won when a team gains 15 points with a 2 point lead.

The venues for this sport are the *Sant Jordi Hall* and the *Barcelona Sports Hall*.

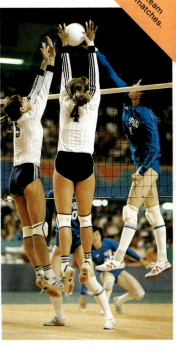

VOLLEYBALL...RESULTS...

	1988 winner	1992 winner
Men	USA	_____
Women	URS	_____

WEIGHTLIFTING

The weightlifting competitors are divided into ten weight classes. Each competitor attempts to lift the heaviest possible weight using two different techniques: the *snatch* and the *clean and jerk*. Every weightlifter has up to three attempts at each weight and must succeed in lifting it before attempting a greater weight.

The winner is the competitor who successfully lifts the greatest total weight using both methods of lift. If two competitors tie, both having lifted the same weight, the competitor with the lightest body weight is declared the winner.

The competition will be held at the **L'Espanya Industrial Hall**.

"— OLYMPIC FACTS —"
Harold Sakata (USA) won the silver medal in the 82.5 kg class in 1948. He later starred as "Oddjob" in the James Bond film Goldfinger.

Yuri Zakharevich (URS), gold medallist in the 110 kg weight class

In the snatch, the competitor must lift the bar with both hands to arm's length above his head. This must be done in one continuous movement

WEIGHTLIFTING...RESULTS...

Weight class	Olympic record and result	1988 winner and result	1992 winner and result
Up to 52 kg	S Marinov (BUL) 270 kg	S Marinov (BUL) 270 kg	
Up to 56 kg	O Mirzoyan (URS) 292.5 kg	O Mirzoyan (URS) 292.5 kg	
Up to 60 kg	N Suleymanoglu (TUR) 342.5 kg	N Suleymanoglu (TUR) 342.5 kg	
Up to 67.5 kg	Y Rusev (BUL) 342.5 kg	J Kunz (GDR) 340 kg	
Up to 75 kg	B Guidikov (BUL) 375 kg	B Guidikov (BUL) 375 kg	
Up to 82.5 kg	Y Vardanyan (URS) 400 kg	I Arsamakov (URS) 377.5 kg	
Up to 90 kg	A Khrapatiy (URS) 412.5 kg	A Khrapatiy (URS) 412.5 kg	
Up to 100 kg	P Kuznetsov (URS) 425 kg	P Kuznetsov (URS) 425 kg	
Up to 110 kg	Y Zakharevich (URS) 455 kg	Y Zakharevich (URS) 455 kg	
Over 110 kg	A Kurlovich (URS) 462.5 kg	A Kurlovich (URS) 462.5 kg	

WRESTLING

Two forms of wrestling are contested at the Olympic Games: *freestyle* and *Greco-Roman*. In the Greco-Roman form the use of legs is restricted.

Each bout takes place on a 12 m (39ft 4¼in) square mat and consists of a single period of five minutes. If both wrestlers have the same score at the end of this time the referee orders an extension of the bout until one wrestler scores a winning technical point.

The competition venue is the new **National Institute of Physical Education**.

«—OLYMPIC FACTS—»
The longest wrestling bout in Olympic history was between Martin Klein (URS) and Alfred Asikainen (FIN) in 1912. It lasted for 11 hours and 40 minutes.

WRESTLING...RESULTS...

Weight class	1988 winner	1992 winner
Freestyle		
Up to 48 kg (Light flyweight)	T Kobayashi (JPN)	
Up to 52 kg (Flyweight)	M Sato (JPN)	
Up to 57 kg (Bantamweight)	S Beloglazov (URS)	
Up to 62 kg (Featherweight)	J Smith (USA)	
Up to 68 kg (Lightweight)	A Fadzayev (URS)	
Up to 74 kg (Welterweight)	K Monday (USA)	
Up to 82 kg (Middleweight)	H Myung-Woo (KOR)	
Up to 90 kg (Light heavyweight)	M Khadartsev (URS)	
Up to 100 kg (Heavyweight)	V Puscasu (ROM)	
Up to 130 kg (Super-heavyweight)	D Gabedjichvli (URS)	
Greco-Roman		
Up to 48 kg (Light flyweight)	V Maenza (ITA)	
Up to 52 kg (Flyweight)	J Ronningen (NOR)	
Up to 57 kg (Bantamweight)	A Sike (HUN)	
Up to 62 kg (Featherweight)	K Madjidov (URS)	
Up to 68 kg (Lightweight)	L Djoulfalakian (URS)	
Up to 74 kg (Welterweight)	K Young-Nam (KOR)	
Up to 82 kg (Middleweight)	M Mamiachvli (URS)	
Up to 90 kg (Light heavyweight)	A Komchev (BUL)	
Up to 100 kg (Heavyweight)	A Wronski (POL)	
Up to 130 kg (Super-heavyweight)	A Kareline (URS)	

YACHTING

The regatta consists of eight different international classes. In four of these classes (Soling, Flying Dutchman, Star and Tornado), the crews can be made up of men or women. In the 470 and Lechner A-390 classes, men and women compete in different events. In addition, there is a Finn class for men and a Europe class for women. In each class (except soling) there are seven races over a set course. The best six results from the seven races count towards the final medal placings. In soling the top six competitors from a six-race match move on to a round robin competition, where each competitor races all the others once. Then the top four teams move on to semi-finals and finals.

The yachting events will be held at the ***Olympic Harbour***.

The 470 class; Seoul, 1988

The 1988 British team; men's 470 class

YACHTING...RESULTS...

Class	1988 winner	1992 winner
Open		
Soling (keelboat)	GDR	
Star (keelboat)	GBR	
Flying Dutchman (centreboard dinghy)	DEN	
Tornado (catamaran)	NZL	
Men		
Lechner A-390 (sailboard)	§*New event*	
470 (centreboard dinghy)	FRA	
Finn (centreboard dinghy)	*New event	
Women		
Lechner A-390 (sailboard)	§*New event*	
470 (centreboard dinghy)	USA	
Europe (centreboard dinghy)	*New event*	

*The Finn was a single open class event in 1988, when it was won by Spain
§The Lechner A-390 replaces the Division II, which was won in 1988 by B Kendall (NZL)

World records

Athletics – Track and Field*

Men's events	Record	Holder	Date
100 m	9.86	Carl Lewis (USA)	1991
200 m	19.72	Pietro Mennea (ITA)	1979
400 m	43.29	Harry Reynolds (USA)	1988
800 m	1:41.73	Sebastian Coe (GBR)	1981
1,500 m	3:29.46	Said Aouita (MAR)	1985
5,000 m	12:58.39	Said Aouita (MAR)	1987
10,000 m	27:08.23	Arturo Barrios (MEX)	1989
4 x 100 m relay	37.50	USA	1991
4 x 400 m relay	2:56.16	USA	1968
110 m hurdles	12.92	Roger Kingdom (USA)	1989
400 m hurdles	47.02	Edwin Moses (USA)	1983
3,000 m st'chase	8:05.35	Peter Koech (KEN)	1989
20 km walk	1:18:40	Ernesto Canto (MEX)	1984
50 km walk	3:41:38	Raul Gonzales (MEX)	1979
High jump	2.44 m	Javier Sotomayor (CUB)	1989
Long jump	8.95 m	Mike Powell (USA)	1991
Pole vault	6.10 m	Sergey Bubka (URS)	1991
Triple jump	17.97 m	Willie Banks (USA)	1985
Shot	23.12 m	Randy Barnes (USA)	1990
Discus	74.08 m	Jurgen Schult (GDR)	1986
Hammer	86.74 m	Yuriy Sedykh (URS)	1986